STILL POINT MEDITATIONS

FOR SCHOOL AND PARISH

Tim Quinlan

Published 2002 by
Veritas Publications
7/8 Lower Abbey Street
Dublin 1
Email publications@veritas.ie
Website www.veritas.ie

ISBN 1 85390 606 9

All Scripture quotes, unless otherwise credited, quoted from the *Good News Bible* published by the Bible Societies/HarperCollins Publishers Ltd, UK, © American Bible Society, 1966, 1971, 1976, 1992. Psalm 8 (in Meditation 7) quoted from the *New Revised Standard Version Bible: Catholic Edition* © 1993 and 1989 by the Division of Christian Education of the National Council of the Churches of Christ in the USA. Used by permission; all rights reserved. Extract from *St Patrick Writes* by Joseph Duffy, DD (Irish Messenger Publications, 1980).

A catalogue record for this book is available from the British Library.

Designed by Colette Dower
Printed in the Republic of Ireland by Criterion Press, Dublin

Veritas books are printed on paper made from the wood pulp of managed forests. For every tree felled, at least one tree is planted, thereby renewing natural resources.

Contents

Introduction   5

Suggested Scripture Texts   17

Meditations

    1 – *New Beginnings*   20

    2 – *Autumn*   22

    3 – *My Gifts*   24

    4 – *Rest & Renewal*   26

    5 – *Sharing a Problem*   28

    6 – *Sickness*   30

    7 – *The Blue Planet*   32

    8 – *The Family*   34

    9 – *Advent 1*   36

    10 – *Advent 2*   38

    11 – *Advent 3*   40

    12 – *Advent 4*   42

    13 – *Epiphany/Journey/Prince of Peace* 44

    14 – *Exam Time*   46

    15 – *Wet, Gloomy Day*   48

    16 – *Winter*   50

    17 – *In the Eye of the Storm*   52

    18 – *Doubt*   54

    19 – *Forgiveness*   56

    20 – *Healing*   58

    21 – *Journey*   60

    22 – *Spring*   62

    23 – *Desert (Lent 1)*   64

    24 – *Our Desire for God (Lent 2)*   66

    25 – *Repentance (Lent 3)*   68

    26 – *Trust (Lent 4)*   70

    27 – *Meal/Eucharist/Holy Thursday*   72

    28 – *Suffering/Passion/Good Friday*   74

    29 – *New Life/Resurrection/Easter Sunday* 76

    30 – *Light*   78

31 – *Water*   80

32 – *Summer*   82

33 – *Earth (Clay)*   84

34 – *Air (Spirit)*   86

35 – *Fire*   88

36 – *Edmund Rice (Inspirational Character)*   90

37 – *St Patrick*   92

38 – *St Brigid*   94

Bibliography   96

Resources on the Internet   99

Introduction

Having taught Religious Education for over twenty years, I have long been aware not alone of the popularity of meditative and reflective exercises, but of their deeply enriching potential. In a world that is fraught with tension, stress and pressure, oases of peace, quiet and calm are a necessity. The same is true of the smaller world of education which mirrors so much the larger one – from the pressures of examinations to an overcrowded curriculum, not to mention the other stressors such as family life, marriage breakdown, poverty, illness and the struggle with the traffic every morning to arrive on time at our places of work and schools. Meditative exercises consequently have an important role to play in helping us all to enter the still centre of our own being, in becoming calm and relaxed and ready to meet the day with a better and healthier attitude.

This little book came about as the result of the suggestion of a colleague of mine, Ms. Mairead Martin, who has taught with me for a number of years. Most of the exercises in this book have been tried with our students at St Joseph's and have been found useful. It is our hope that you will find them just as beneficial in your working life – as a teacher, parent or group leader – and as rewarding for those whom it is your privilege to guide through the meditations.

What is Meditation?

The word 'meditation' has been bandied about so much in the last thirty years or so that a certain amount of confusion exists as to what it is. Today, most people use the terms 'meditation' and 'contemplation' interchangeably. From a traditional and devotional Catholic viewpoint there would have been a distinct difference between these two words, with the former denoting a mental exercise of reading over and pondering a set religious text, while the latter would refer to a higher and more mystical process quite similar to what we mean by 'meditation' today. For our purposes here, I am using the term to denote any practice that helps the individual to centre herself, to become more aware of her own spiritual core, and in the final analysis to enter into the presence of God in her own innermost heart. In short, when I use the term 'meditation' in this text, I also embrace the meanings of the terms 'prayer' and 'contemplation'.

Practically all alternative and complementary health movements and practices recommend meditation in the general sense. It is practised widely in counselling and therapy, both in workshops and on an individual basis. Many distinguished psychiatrists, psychologists and doctors recommend it to help their patients on the journey to healing.[1] Indeed, there are several forms of meditative practices, but in this little book I refer to meditation as the act of relaxing or quieting the body so as to enter into the silence within, to enter one's inner being as it were. This, I hasten to add is a first step on a different, deeper journey for a Christian. To this extent anybody of any religion or none can engage in this sort of meditative practice. I remember Fr William Johnson SJ, a great contemporary Christian mystic and meditator of our age, mentioning at a conference some years back that his meditation group at Sophia University in Tokyo had Christian, Shinto, agnostic, atheist and Buddhist meditators.[2] This struck me as heartening and ecumenical in the broadest sense of that term. There are many forms of meditation, but they all use concentration techniques, which help to stop thoughts, distractions and other concerns that may be racing around our mind. When the mind is calm, like a lake without any ripples, we experience total peace and empowerment.

There is indeed much common ground between all races and religions, and even those of our fellows who are unbelievers. This should not surprise us as we have a shared humanity reaching ever beyond us for some glimmers of meaning in a world that can be all too dismal and depressing at times. However, Christianity as it grew up in the West had a tradition of meditative practice, which it had somehow forgotten over more recent centuries. We have only to recall *The Cloud of Unknowing*: a fourteenth century Christian work on meditation, which is well worth reading and exploring.[3] More recently, we can point to the late Benedictine monk Fr John Main who did a lot in his life to promote Christian meditation through the use of mantra techniques, a tradition that is now widely promoted by his confrère Fr Lawrence Freeman OSB.[4] Others, too, can be mentioned like Anthony de Mello SJ, Mark Link SJ and – still another Jesuit – Fr William Johnston to whom we have alluded above.[5] Nearer to home, we can advert to the great work of Monsignor G. T. Fehily of Dun Laoghaire in promoting Christian meditation by organising national and international conferences on prayer and meditation and by setting up not alone a meditation group in his parish, but by founding *The Christian Meditation Centre.*[6]

Thankfully we also have a profusion of books and tapes widely available for everyday use, but none to my knowledge that offers a sequence of meditative fantasies contained within the covers of one book, which can be used profitably within the context of a school year or over a sustained number of weeks by a prayer/meditation group. The object of this book is to fill that gap in the market.

Some Preliminary Practical Points

(a) *Read through the meditations.* It is strongly recommended that the teacher or facilitator reads through each meditation before attempting it so that minor changes may be made to render them more suitable to the group in question. Such minor changes might be the substitution of 'end of term exams' for 'Junior or Leaving Certificate Exams', or the adaption of a meditation to reflect the environment and family situation of their own students. It would also be beneficial for the teacher or leader to discuss the particular theme with the class before beginning in case there are any aspects that might be upsetting, or that the students might find difficult to understand. Themes such as suffering and illness need to be handled sensitively by the teacher.

(b) *List of Scripture texts:* I have also included a list of Scripture texts with relevant themes highlighted immediately before the meditation section. The teacher or leader may wish to pick a different text from this selection instead of the one given in the Scriptural section of the meditation. Of course, you may substitute any relevant text of your own choice that has not been included in this list.

(c) *Meditation places*: Those of you who have an oratory in your school or parish are really blessed as you can make the atmosphere really special and pleasant. With an oratory you are well along the way to running a successful meditation practice. However, with a little effort it can also be profitably done in a small room with ordinary sturdy chairs or even in a classroom with wooden desks. This last situation is the hardest, but with a little effort like finding a room away from the throb of school life, or even putting a 'Do Not Disturb' notice on the door, one can run a successful meditation session. Students/participants should be encouraged to attempt meditation on their own too in their bedroom, a little-used room in their home or even in a secluded place outdoors. The important thing is to get the praying space right, as it is one of the keys to effective meditation.

(d) *Meditation times:* Firstly, a word for teachers. At school I have often found either the first or last class periods in the day effective. Don't worry if any pupils fall asleep – that happens to the best meditator at times. Also caution the students not to interfere with or interrupt any other student, pointing out that this a special time for them to get in touch with themselves before they open themselves to entering the presence of the Lord. Knowing whether a class is ready or not for meditation is also crucial. In other words, there is no substitute for getting to know your class well. A good teacher will know instinctively when and where and at what time to do an exercise in this area. However, be prepared to fail a few times too. This is the surest way to learn! A Parish group, unlike its school counterpart, will be able to select the most suitable time to meet.

(e) *Pace of speaker/leader:* If you are leading a meditation, pace is crucial – it must be slow, slow, slow, with plenty of appropriate pauses. Get used to hearing your own voice and living with silence. It's the silences and pauses that do most of the work, not the voice, rather like a Beckett drama. After each sentence, allow an appropriate pause to help the participant to visualise what's being said.

(f) *Posture:* In Zen practice control of the body is a preliminary essential. Eastern religions know how to put the body at the service of prayer. In the final analysis, the best posture is the one that helps you pray. However, for the purposes of a facilitated meditation at school or in the parish sitting erect in a chair with the back straight, both feet flat on the floor and hands in your lap or on the desktop is to be preferred. There are some people who are able to sit with legs crossed either in the half-lotus or full-lotus position, but these are the experts. With a lot of practice we may get there too!

(g) *Breathing:* Observing the breath or the very process of breathing has long been a basic method of meditation in the East. The task here is to get the participant to breathe smoothly, deeply and slowly. Such a pattern, once achieved, inevitably leads to more effective and deeper meditation. Such a concentration is at the heart of all meditation.

(h) *Listening:* Another essential of meditation is that of *awareness.* Awareness can best be achieved by learning to listen: to one's own body, thoughts and feelings. We start by listening to the sounds outside the room, then the ones inside the room, then the very slight sounds in our own body (small movements, our breath, our stomach and our heart). By focusing initially on outside sounds they will eventually cease to distract us – we have already given our attention to them and so we can let go of them all the more easily.

(i) *Use of the senses:* We have already alluded to hearing/listening. In any meditation exercise we use the sense of touch also, we become aware of the feel of the seat under us or of the touch of our clothes. We might even use the sense of smell insofar as we might use incense or some other aroma to produce a relaxing atmosphere. We can, of course, engage in a meditative exercise using our eyesight by focusing on a candle, icon or image. This works best in an oratory or a classroom where the desks have been cleared away, as too much clutter can distract the students' focus. The candle has always been a central religious and spiritual symbol. The Eastern religions often refer to a special meditation using special images as *Yantras.* Yantras are ancient geometrical designs that are doorways into deeper awareness. The practice of focusing the mind on something external or internal helps to make the mind quiet. The Russian and Greek Orthodox Christian Churches have long used icons in such a fashion. As any artist will tell you, the very process of creating an icon is itself a form of meditation. So objects and images can be profitably used in any meditative exercise. This list includes candles, incense, various aromas, icons, pictures, stones, shells, leaves, acorns, branches, twigs, turf, water – in short, any object or image from nature that can make up a centrepiece for a meditation exercise.

(j)   *Mantra:* One important technique is the use of the mantra. Mantras are sacred words or phrases, the shorter the better, which, when repeated either out loud or in our mind, help to bring the individual into a deeper sense of self, or into a higher state of consciousness, or into deeper spiritual awareness or more closely into a sense of the presence of God – obviously a Christian would use this last formulation, though each of the other formulations are necessary stepping stones to a deeper religious experience from a theological point of view. Without a doubt, Taizé prayer uses the repeated mantra and it is correctly called a form of meditation, as indeed would the Rosary and other ancient litanies and certainly Gregorian Chant. Truly, there is nothing new under the sun. Chanting a mantra repeatedly for the duration of your meditation session will, over time, develop your powers of meditation to a high degree. Each time your mind is distracted from pure concentration, bring it back by repeatedly returning to your mantra. *Om Mani Padme Hum* or 'Enlightenment is within everything' is a traditional Hindu and Buddhist mantra and is extremely ancient. A Christian mantra might be any phrase the meditator or facilitator might choose like 'Jesus is Lord of Life' or 'My Lord and My God', i.e., any short scriptural or theological phrase. It is often beneficial to say the mantra on the inward or outward breaths or on both.

(k)   *Use of Scripture:* The Bible has long been a source for much meditation and prayer. We need only recall the great communal prayers of the Old Testament, found in The Book of Psalms, essentially the prayer book of the ancient Jewish community, and they run the whole gamut of emotions and religious sentiments from dejection and despair through anger and pain to trust and hope in the Lord of Life. Since they encompass such a broad range of emotions and sentiments, the psalms, or appropriate sections of them, are most suitable for meditation. Likewise with the rest of Scripture, especially the Gospel stories. St Ignatius of Loyola spearheaded a form of prayer known as 'The Exercises of St Ignatius', which allowed the meditator to imaginatively place him or herself in the Gospel story. Another version of Scriptural prayer would be what is now popularly called *Lectio divina* which focuses on four basic movements in praying the Scriptures, namely *lectio* (reading), *meditatio* (meditation), *oratio* (prayer) and *contemplatio* (contemplation).[7]

(l) *Use of music:* This probably does not need to be mentioned, but the use of relaxing music during a meditation or a fantasy session can be most helpful in creating a relaxing and conducive atmosphere. There is a wide variety of tapes and CDs readily available.

(m) *Use of story:* A favourite story can also be used profitably for the second phase of a meditation, that is, the fantasy part. Jesus himself was a great storyteller because he realised their teaching potential. So having a good repertoire of favourite stories is very beneficial.

(n) *Duration of a session:* For absolute beginners a five to ten minute session is recommended. Initially I have found it most beneficial to introduce beginners to the relaxation part of the exercise only for a few sessions. Then, I'd gradually lengthen the session to involve a fantasy exercise. Eventually, when they are used to the technique involved, one can lead them into a Scripture meditation. I have found that half an hour is actually a maximum, from a school point of view at least. A fifteen to twenty minute session is often the ideal.

(o) *Use of the Internet:* There are many useful sites on the World-Wide Web dedicated to meditation and spirituality, which endeavour to bring a sense of the spiritual to the modem world – and indeed, some of them will actually lead you through an exercise in meditation. I have given a list of some of these sites at the back of the book.

Structure of these Meditations

All the meditations in this book mostly conform to the following pattern:

(1) *Introduction – Relaxing the body:* In this section we use the quieting and relaxation techniques common to most forms of meditation, which start by relaxing the body first through an awareness of the five senses and then seek to still the thoughts and the feelings.

(2) *Meditation/Fantasy proper:* Next we lead the 'meditator' on a journey in imagination or fantasy, which seeks to make him or her more mindful or aware of the deeper issues in life.

(3) *Scripture:* Then we introduce some Scriptural text, which can be entered into in a more imaginative and consequently more dynamic way.

(4) *Conclusion:* We conclude by bringing our attention back to the body and its rhythmic breathing and then gently lead the meditator back to a fully conscious awareness of his/her surroundings.

The first and final parts of the above process are naturally quite formulaic. Two sample introductions and endings are given here, but the facilitator may use any other combination of words he/she may wish so as to bring the meditator into a relaxed state and finally out of that state into an awareness of their surroundings. The teacher or facilitator may choose to use just three movements instead of the longer four in any meditation exercise by choosing to use just one of the two sections (2) or (3), i.e., either the Fantasy or the Scriptural section.

Each reflection, then, in this book will begin with an introduction, i.e., a relaxation exercise. The following are two possible such introductions to any of the meditations offered in this book.

Introduction 1

Times of silence are precious. Our aim is to enter into silence – the silence of our own hearts. To do so, we must first become relaxed. Throughout this exercise we ask everyone to refrain from any unnecessary movement. In order to become still in our innermost heart we must first become still in our body.

And so, firstly we relax our bodies. Just close your eyes gently. Bring your attention to your neck and shoulders. Notice any tension you experience there, and just imagine that tension flowing gently down your arms and out of your body through your fingers.

Become aware of your back against the seat and then, further down, feel your weight pressing against the seat. You are becoming more and more relaxed.

You are now breathing nice and easily. Bring your attention to your breath, but don't breathe any more heavily than you normally do. Notice the colder air at the bottom of your nostrils as you breathe in, and the warmer air as you breathe out.

The breath you are breathing now is the breath of life; the breath that God breathed into your body when you were born. Remember, you are the receiver of this breath of life, not its giver.

OR

Introduction 2

(a) Relaxing the Body:
   We are now going to get into a relaxed and comfortable position, and once we get to that point, we avoid any unnecessary shifting or moving. If someone does have to move throughout the session, do so as gently as possible so as not to disturb others. First, gently close your eyes. Sit straight in the chair or desk, leaning comfortably against the back. Both feet are flat on the floor. Rest your hands gently on your knees or hold them together loosely. Stay just as you are now and we'll go over all that again.

(b) Relaxing the Mind:
   Now we are going to relax the mind. Images and thoughts will come into your mind – just let them come and go gently. Don't focus on any thought or image in particular. Just let them come and go of their own accord. All is very gentle. There is no tension or stress. You are becoming more and more relaxed.

(c) Relaxing the Feelings:
   Our feelings come and go, just like the waves of the sea. We're very much aware of their presence. You may be angry with someone. You may be a little sad or depressed, or you may be happy and full of life. Just be aware of how you feel. Just relax and let those feelings go. There is no strain or stress. All is gentle and calm and you are becoming still more relaxed.

(d) Becoming Aware:
   We are now going to become aware of our bodies. As I go through this exercise, just let your attention float to focus on the part of the body being brought to awareness: become aware of your neck and your shoulders.

Feel your shirt collar and clothes pressing against them. Become aware of your back and feel it resting against the back of the chair. Become aware of your arms and hands. Feel them resting on your knees or against the desk. As you are so relaxed you can feel your heart beating gently. For a moment now, see if you can find and stay with your heartbeat.

(e) Breathing:
Become aware of your breathing. Don't breathe any more heavily or deeply than you normally do. Just become aware of your breathing. As you breathe in you feel the colder air enter your nostrils, going down your throat and into your lungs. As you breathe out, you feel the warmer air coming out of your lungs, up through my throat and out through your nostrils. This is the breath of life. You did not create it. The Lord of Life breathed it into you at your birth. Give thanks for this breath. Give thanks for this gift of life.

This second introduction is somewhat longer, so, if desired, the leader or facilitator can add his or her own prayers or mantras after the breathing exercise, omit sections (b) and (c) and then go on then to the conclusion of the prayer. Alternatively, they may choose to use one of the Fantasy or Scripture sections with a shortened introduction. The teacher or facilitator will find the most suitable format for themselves and their group.

Conclusion

This is obviously the shortest part of the fourfold movement of the meditation process, but it is also very important. The meditator is totally relaxed and at a deeper level of consciousness, so he or she has to be brought gently back to an awareness of the room and the surroundings. Below, I give two possible conclusions:

Conclusion (1)

Return your attention now to your breath. Notice how peacefully you are breathing. Become aware of your body and your posture as you sit in your seat. Listen to the sounds in the room and those from outside. Gradually open your eyes and begin to stretch gently.

OR

Conclusion (2)

Once again, become aware of your body. Become aware of your position in the seat. Bring your attention to your breathing. Notice how calm and relaxed and peaceful it is. Begin now to stretch your arms and your legs. Open your eyes gently and become aware of the room and the people around you.

Notes

1. Dr Bernie S. Siegel, a medical practitioner and surgeon, has used meditation techniques with some success with cancer patients. Such techniques have also been used effectively in a wide variety of psychotherapies from Jungian Analysis to holistic counselling. Dr Dorothy Rowe, a psychologist, highly recommends it for patients battling against depression. For more information please refer to the bibliography.

2. Fr Johnston's latest book on meditation is *Arise My Love: Mysticism for a New Era* (Orbis Books, 2000). This book is at once a powerful reflection on the movement of interfaith dialogue and the re-discovery of Christianity's own mystical origins. Fr Johnston has said '...we have a long, rich and soundly based tradition of mystical prayer in the Catholic Church. However, except for the enclosed monasteries and convents, we ceased teaching it in our seminaries early in the twentieth century.'

3. This treatise by an anonymous English mystic of the late fourteenth century is one of the classics on contemplative prayer in the Christian tradition. Its contents centre on practical advice on how to meditate. Similar counsel is to be found in John of the Cross, Jan van Ruysbroeck, John Tauler and, much earlier, in St Augustine and Richard of St Victor. There is no paucity of Christian texts on meditation – unfortunately, they are just less well known than their Buddhist, Hindu or Zen counterparts.

4. John Main OSB (1926-1982) was born in London and discovered the Christian tradition of the mantra through his reading of the early Christian monks, especially John Cassian. He went on to teach this type of meditative prayer with mantra from within the rich context of Christian Scripture and theology. Laurence Freeman OSB is a successor to John Main and has been directing *The World Community For Christian Meditation* since 1992. For information on his books see the bibliography.

5. Anthony de Mello SJ, was renowned for his efforts to bring the spiritual fruits of the East to the men and women of the West. As a native of India, he was well placed to produce a unique and enriching synthesis of the best of both worlds as regards

prayer, meditation and contemplation. Please refer to the Bibliography for further information. More recently, the Jesuit, Fr John Callanan has been de Mello's great interpreter in Ireland. The American, Mark Link SJ, an American, has been a best selling author in the area of prayer and meditation for many years now. He also has his own website dedicated to prayer and meditation. Please refer to bibliography.

6. Contact Address: *The Christian Meditation Centre*, 4 Eblana Avenue, Dún Laoghaire, Co. Dublin, Tel. 353 1 2801505/353 1 2807827/353 1 2804969

7. For a good account of the process of *Lectio divina* see *Spirituality* Volume 1, numbers 1 and 2, which has an excellent introduction by Michel de Verteuil CSSp, and *Eucharist as Word* by Michel de Verteuil CSSp (Veritas 2001). See also *Spirituality*, Volume 3, number 15 and Volume 4, number 16 for two excellent articles by Cardinal Carlo Maria Montini on *Lectio divina* and vocation in life.

Suggested Scripture Texts

N.B. In texts where the second person singular is used, the facilitator could profitably ask the participants to substitute their own Christian name for 'you' in the text. In the suggested texts below the second person is italicised as an aide memoire. Obviously, the list is not exhaustive, but it may prove helpful.

Text	Themes
Genesis 1:27 –31	*You* are in the image and likeness of God.
Ephesians 2:22	*You* are my work of art. (you are very special)
Ephesians 1:2-3	*You* have many blessings in Christ.
Corinthians 3:18	*You* reflect Christ.
Ephesians 1:2-3	I chose *you* in Christ.
Psalm 8.5	I made *you* a little less than the angels.
John 31:3	I have loved *you* with an everlasting love.
Psalm 23	*You* shall not want. (The Lord is my Shepherd).
Ephesians 3:17	I am silently planning for *you* in love.
Isaiah 43	I have called *you* by your name.
Isaiah 43	*You* are precious in my eyes.
Luke 12:28	*You* are worth more than many sparrows.
Isaiah 49:16	*Your* name is carved on the palm of my hand.
Galatians 2:20	I loved *you*.
1 Corinthians 20	*You* are not your own property.
1 Corinthians 6:19	*You* are a temple of the Holy Spirit.
2 Corinthians 5	*You* have become the goodness of God.

2 Corinthians 1:20	I set *you* apart.
1 John 3:2	*You* shall become like me.
Revelations 22:4	*You* shall see me face to face.
Mark 1:9 –11	I am very pleased with *you*. (Love/belonging).
Matthew 5:23-24	Leave your gift before the altar. (Forgiveness).
Luke 6; 37-38	Do not judge others.
Matthew 7:24- 27	Sound foundations. (Security in the Lord.)
Mark 8:1-4	Jesus feeds the hungry... feels sorry...
John 6:35	I am the Bread of Life.
Matthew 18:1-5 (Mark 10:13-16)	Innocence, trust and acceptance (like children).
Matthew 18:12-14 (Luke 15:4-8)	The Lost Sheep, the Lord rejoices.
Matthew 18:21-22	Forgiveness, seventy times seven.
Matthew 11:28-30	Acceptance, belonging, support.
Luke 10:30-37	The Good Samaritan.
John 10:11-15	The Good Shepherd.
Mark 10:17-21	The Rich Young Man, Cost of Discipleship.
Luke 15:11-33	The Prodigal Son.
Luke 16:19-21, 19:1- 10	The theme of poverty, sharing, true riches.
John 11:21-35	The raising of Lazarus... Jesus wept.
Matthew 25:14-30	Using our talents.
Luke 21:1-4	The widow's mite. (Generosity).
Mark 2:13-17	I have come to heal the sick (sinners).
Luke 14:28-30	Good preparation for the future is essential.

Meditations

Meditation 1: New Beginnings

Introduction

Either of those given on pp. 12, 13 and 14 or one
of the leader's choice

Meditation/Fantasy

In your imagination cast your mind back to your first day at
school. See if you can recapture the sense of expectation and the
excitement of that day. In your mind's eye, paint how you looked
on that occasion, how your friends looked, how the school
looked. Life is a series of new beginnings and starts. Nothing
stays the same. Things move on.

Now is the start of another new beginning for each of us, our
first year in secondary school. In your mind allow the images of
all the experiences of your new school to come and go. Life is a
series of new things, new subjects, new hobbies, new sports,
and, especially, new friends. One by one bring to mind all these
new subjects, sports and friends.

Moving on can be tough too. New subjects bring difficulties.
New buildings seem strange and sometimes frightening. Our
teachers are there to help. Call them to mind now. Our friends
are there to help. Call them to mind now. There are probably a
good number of them in who you would trust and in who you
could confide if you were in trouble. Call them to mind. Think
also of the friends that you laughed with in the yard this morning
before coming to class. Call that sense of fun to mind now.

We give thanks for all the good things in our lives and for all the new experiences we will have over the coming year. We look forward to them with expectation. We give thanks for the gift of life, for the breath we are breathing now, the breath of life.

Conclusion

Once again, become aware of your breathing. Do not breathe any more heavily than you have been doing thus far. Become aware of the colder air at the bottom of your nostrils as you breathe in and the warmer air as you breathe out. Stay with your breath now for a few moments. Once again become aware of your surroundings, the noises inside and outside of the room. Open your eyes.

Meditation 2: Autumn

Introduction

Either of those given on pp. 12, 13 and 14 or one of the leader's choice

Meditation/Fantasy

Autumn is a very colourful and pleasant season. Imagine now that you are walking down a country lane. The leaves on the trees are a myriad of colours: yellow, red, brown and rust-coloured. The ground is muddy and your shoes are spattered. There are fallen leaves everywhere. There is only a very slight chill in the wind, and there are still leaves on the trees that have not yet fallen. The sun is low in the sky and is glinting through the half-bare branches.

On the one hand there is the spring of new growth in delicate buds, and the fulsome blossoms of summertime, on the other there is the dying back of autumn and the death of winter. It is the same for all life, as well as for nature. Plants grow, mature and die. Animals grow, mature and die. We all grow, mature and die. Autumn is a season of maturing, but also of a certain dying to reach that maturity.

As you walk, notice again the leaves under foot and their many shades of yellows and browns. Notice other leaves as they fall in the wind. Notice the forlorn leaves that have yet to fall. Are there any things that are falling away or changing in your life at the moment? Are you coming near any turning point in your life like sitting the Junior or Leaving Cert? Are there people who are going to go away or fall away as friends? Notice how life continually changes. Notice how the cycle of new life, dying, death and new life again goes on and on.

Our autumn is really a beautiful time, a time of achieved growth and maturity. There have been many little deaths, like failures at study, lack of success in the league and illnesses in the family. But from all these little deaths we have learnt and have come to a maturity of acceptance. New growth will begin next spring at the spot where the old leaves have fallen away.

Conclusion

Either of the ones given on p. 15 or one of the leader's choice

Meditation 3: My Gifts

Introduction

Either of those given on pp. 12, 13 and 14 or one of the leader's choice

Meditation/Fantasy

Imagine now that you are walking into a theatre. Describe it in your mind's eye. See yourself walking up to the very first row. There is no one else in the theatre. You sit down and look at the stage... Gradually the curtains open to reveal a large armchair in the middle of the stage. Imagine now a big leather armchair.

Eventually your favourite hero or heroine comes out onto the stage and sits down. Name this person in your mind. Describe how this person looks, how he or she is dressed. You start to talk to this person telling him or her all the things you admire about them – think of all the gifts that this talented individual has.

This person gets up after a while and bids you goodbye. Then another person comes out onto the stage and sits down. After a while, you realise that this second person is you yourself. Describe how you look, how you are dressed. Now tell yourself all the good things you admire about YOU! Think of all the gifts and talents that you possess as a unique human being.

See yourself now, getting up from the front row and going up on the stage to meet yourself. Shake hands with this new, personal you. Perhaps even hug him or her.

Scriptural Reflection

There are different kinds of spiritual gifts, but the same Spirit gives them. There are different ways of serving, but the same Lord is served. There are different abilities to perform services, but the same God gives ability to all for their particular service. The Spirit's presence is shown in some way in each person for the good of all. The Spirit gives one person a message full of wisdom, while to another person the same Spirit gives a message full of knowledge. One and the same Spirit gives faith to one person, while to another person he gives the power to heal. The Spirit gives one person the power to work miracles; to another the gift of speaking God's message; and to yet another, the ability to tell the difference between gifts that come from the Spirit and those which do not. To one person he gives the ability to speak in strange tongues, and to another he gives the ability to explain what is said. But it is the one Spirit who does all this; as he wishes, he gives a different gift to each person.

1 CORINTHIANS 12:4-11

Conclusion

Either of the ones given on p. 15 or one of the leader's choice

Meditation 4: Rest & Renewal

Introduction

Either of those given on pp. 12, 13 and 14 or one of the leader's choice

Meditation/Fantasy

Imagine now that you have just finished a long session of training, a hard game of tennis, an energetic workout, a hectic match or a long run. Call to mind the feeling of tiredness yet satisfaction. It's great to have used up all that excess energy, but you are quite drained. Imagine the refreshing shower afterwards.

Now imagine that you are going to your favourite outdoor place. It is a sunny day and you are going to relax and lie back in the sun. Paint in all the physical details of the location where you are. Feel the warmth of the sun's rays gently bathing your face and limbs. Feel the fresh air on your nostrils as you breathe in.

It is great to relax and rest. We need these moments, moments when we just get away from everything and from everyone; moments when we get a chance to unwind and just *be*. Just breathe gently and *relax*.

Imagine now that you are back in New Testament times, in Palestine at the time of Jesus. It is a hot and sandy place. Jesus turns to his disciples – and you are one of them – and he invites all of you to come away with him to the hilltop or mountainside, to get away from the crowds after a long day preaching and healing. Picture this scene. You all sit down on the hillside and Jesus says the following words to you:

Scriptural Reflection

Ask and you shall receive; seek and you shall find; knock and the door shall be opened for you. For everyone who asks shall receive, and anyone who seeks shall find, and the door shall be opened to him who knocks. Would any of you who are fathers give your son a stone when he asks for bread? Or would you give him a snake when he asks for a fish? Bad as you are, you know how to give good things to your children. How much more, then, will your Father in heaven give good things to those who ask him!

MATTHEW 7:7-11

Conclusion

Either of the ones given on p. 15 or one of the leader's choice

Meditation 5: Sharing A Problem

Introduction

Either of those given on pp. 12, 13 and 14 or one of the leader's choice

Meditation/Fantasy

We all have problems. There is not a person living who has not something to worry about. Call to mind something that has been bothering you recently. Envisage the people involved in this problem. Try to relive that situation now in your imagination.

Now call to mind anybody, any friend or adult or professional, who might be a good listener. Call that person to mind. He or she is a good listener. Call that person by their name in your mind. See yourself coming into that person's presence. See the situation, picture it. Is it indoors or outdoors? Hear yourself now sharing your problem with that person. What does your listener say to you? Perhaps they say nothing?

Now that you have shared your problem, notice how relieved you feel, how that problem has been changed somehow. It will still remain a problem, but now you see that you can do something to improve your situation.

It is often useless and futile to worry. Worrying won't solve our problems. Some form of action will. See yourself taking action, by sharing your problem with another, by taking steps to tackle it.

28

Scriptural Reflection

God is our shelter and strength,
Always ready to help in times of trouble.
So we will not be afraid,
Even if the earth is shaken
And mountains fall into the ocean depths;
Even if the seas roar and rage,
And the hills are shaken with violence…

The Lord Almighty is with us;
The God of Jacob is our refuge.

'Stop your fighting, and know that I am God,
Supreme among the nations,
Supreme over the world!'

The Lord Almighty is with us;
The God of Jacob is our refuge

PSALM 46

Conclusion

Either of the ones given on p. 15 or one of the leader's choice

Meditation 6: Sickness

Introduction

Either of those given on pp. 12, 13 and 14 or one
of the leader's choice

Meditation/Fantasy

It is not easy being sick. Not only do we feel unwell, but also we often lose control over our lives. We find that we cannot do the normal things like play football, cycle our bicycles or go out with friends. We are confined to home, and very often even to our beds. Perhaps someone belonging to you is sick as this very moment. Bring that person to mind. Are they at home or in hospital? What do you think it is like for them?

Cast your mind back to the last time you were really sick and had to stay in bed or even go into hospital. If you have never really been very sick or in hospital, try to imagine what it is like. Picture the corridors of the hospital, the wards, the beds, the nurses and the doctors and all the medical equipment that is about. Try and capture the smells of a hospital if you can.

What do you think you are learning from this experience of being sick?

How precious our health is and yet we really do not appreciate it. We take it for granted. We give thanks for the gift of health that we have here and now, for the ability to walk, to talk, to hear, to see, to smell and to touch, for the health to do all the things we like doing.

Call to mind anyone you know who is sick. Picture them in your mind's eye. Lord we pray for our friend or relative – mention them by name in your mind – that they may be restored to better health. We sit with this person in compassion. Often it is enough to be with someone. There is no need to say too many words. It is often sufficient to sit and share the silence. This is compassion.

Scriptural Reflection

Jesus left that place, and as he walked along, two blind men started following him. 'Take pity on us, Son of David!' they shouted. When Jesus had gone indoors, the two blind men came to him, and he asked them, 'Do you believe that I can heal you?' 'Yes, sir,' they answered. Then Jesus touched their eyes and said 'Let it happen then, just as you believe!' – and their sight was restored. Jesus spoke sternly to them, 'Don't tell this to anyone!' But they left and spread the news about Jesus all over that part of the country.

MATTHEW 9:27–31

Conclusion

Either of the ones given on p. 15 or one of the leader's choice

Meditation 7: The Blue Planet

Introduction

Either of those given on pp. 12, 13 and 14 or one
of the leader's choice

Meditation/Fantasy

Imagine now that you are walking down a pathway towards a
big green field. In the middle of that field there is a huge hot-air
balloon with a basket underneath. Picture the balloon, its colour,
and any advertisements there may be on it. A person comes up
to you and invites you to get into the basket. Gradually, the
sandbag weights are thrown aside and the gas burner is turned
on and the helium released into the balloon. The balloon rises
gradually. Notice how the people on the ground get smaller and
smaller. How the trees become like little plants. How the
roadways are transformed into narrow stripes like coloured lines
on a painting. The balloon is now going higher and higher. You
can see the broad vista of the open country as far as the eye can
manage. You climb up and up, up through the clouds, higher
than the highest mountains until finally you are way up in space.
You look down on the earth and you see a beautiful, blue planet
rotating slowly on its own axis in space. What a beautiful planet
it is. It is our planet earth and it is often called 'The Blue Planet'.

[At this stage in the fantasy, it would be appropriate to play some
classical or meditative music, or the song 'From a Distance' by
Nanci Griffith, if the facilitator so wished.]

Scriptural Reflection

O Lord, our God, how majestic is thy name in all the earth!
Thou whose glory above the heavens is chanted
By the mouths of babes and infants,

When I look at thy heavens, the work of thy fingers,
The moon and the stars which thou hast established;
What is man that thou art mindful of him,
And the son of man that thou dost care for him?
Yet thou hast made him little less than a God,
And dost crown him with glory and honour.
Thou hast given him dominion over the works of thy hands;
Thou hast put all things under his feet,
All sheep, and oxen, and also the beasts of the field,
The birds of the air, and the fish of the sea,
Whatever passes along the paths of the sea.
O lord, our God, how majestic is thy name in all the earth!

PSALM 8

Conclusion

Either of the ones given on p. 15 or one of the leader's choice

Meditation 8: The Family

Introduction

Either of those given on pp. 12, 13 and 14 or one
of the leader's choice

Meditation/Fantasy

Imagine now that it is Sunday afternoon you and your family are
sitting around the dining room table ready to eat your dinner.
Picture in your mind's eye who is sitting where. Go around the
table one by one and name off all the people who are sitting
around the table. These are all the special people in your life.
Remind yourself of the things that each person does for you. Go
through them one by one. Thank God for each of these special
people, for the gift that each one of them is to you.

Is there anyone missing from your table? Gently call that person
to mind. Remember that whether they are gone to their heavenly
reward or are abroad somewhere, they are still present in spirit.
Gently pray for that person. Tell them how much you miss them.
It is healing to call our departed friends and family to mind on
occasion.

Jesus told us that where two or three are gathered in his name
that he himself is there with us. Jesus is also present in a special
way at our tables. When we say grace before or after our meals
we acknowledge that we receive everything including our very
lives as gifts from God. And so now we pray with Jesus by
meditating on the words of the 'Our Father' (Leader recites the
words slowly):

Scriptural Reflection

Our Father who art in heaven,
Hallowed be thy name,
Thy Kingdom come,
Thy will be done,
On earth as it is in heaven,
Give us this day our daily bread;
And forgive us our trespasses
As we forgive those who trespass against us
And lead us not into temptation,
But deliver us from evil.
For if you forgive men their trespasses,
Your heavenly Father also will forgive you;
But if you do not forgive men their trespasses,
Neither will your Father forgive you your trespasses.

MATTHEW 6: 9-14

Conclusion

Either of the ones given on p. 15 or one of the leader's choice

Meditation 9: Advent 1

Introduction

Either of those given on pp. 12, 13 and 14 or one
of the leader's choice

Meditation/Fantasy

Imagine now that you are in a bus or train station. Picture it. It is
sometime around Christmas. Perhaps you are with your family or
friends. Picture them one by one. You are waiting for the arrival
of a favourite uncle, aunt, brother, sister or cousin or some close
family friend. He or she is coming home for a Christmas visit,
perhaps from another town, city or country. In your mind's eye
imagine that scene. In your imagination paint in all your
surroundings – the station, the buses, the trains, the crowds –
and how each of your companions looks. Try and capture how
you would feel. Imagine your expectations. It has been a long
time since you last saw this person. Picture yourself getting up
and greeting this relative or friend. Put yourself in this scene.

All our waiting has been worthwhile. All our expectations have
been realised. Our friend, our uncle, our aunt, our brother, our
sister – call him or her now by name in your mind – has come
home. It is great to have them back in our company for a little
while at least.

Jesus always told stories to bring home his point. One of his great stories is the return home of the Prodigal Son after an absence of many years. The Father in the story is standing out at the gate in the expectation of the arrival home of his long lost son. He sees him in the distance coming down the road. He can't contain his excitement and rushes off to greet him. His son, who was lost, has returned safely home.

In this first week of Advent, we await with hope and expectation the arrival of the Prince of Peace, Jesus the Christ Child into our broken world.

Conclusion

Either of the ones given on p. 15 or one of the leader's choice

Meditation 10: Advent 2

Introduction

Either of those given on pp. 12, 13 and 14 or one of the leader's choice

Meditation/Fantasy

Send yourself back fifty years. Imagine now that you are in a country place, perhaps in the west of Ireland. It is a dark winter's night. Try and picture yourself in a small village or town where there is not much traffic, nor very many shops. Things are not as modern or sophisticated as they are in the city. But old and important customs live on. See yourself, a stranger, walking down the main road of that country village or town, this dark winter's night. Christmas is approaching and traditionally everyone has placed a candle of welcome, welcome for the stranger in the window. You know that if you knock on any door you will be welcomed inside.

Now return in your mind's eye to your own living room. It is time to decorate for Christmas. Name in your imagination all who are there. What each person is doing. What you yourself are doing. See yourself take a candle or a modern stand of electric candles and place it in the window. It is a sign that you and your family will welcome friends, relatives and even strangers to the house this Christmas.

When we open the door of our home to others we are in fact welcoming Jesus into our company. When we help the poor we are in fact welcoming Jesus into our company. When we help the poor we are bringing a little light into their lives. Every time we do good or any little act of kindness we are bringing light into a darkened world. As we prepare for Christmas we wish to open the door of our hearts to others

Conclusion

Either of the ones given on p. 15 or one of the leader's choice

Meditation 11: Advent 3

Introduction

Either of those given on pp. 12, 13 and 14 or one of the leader's choice

Meditation/Fantasy

Recall now any special Christmas moment. Where are you? It could be at school, at the local youth club, in a friend's or a relative's house, perhaps in your own home – it does not matter where. The important thing is to picture that happy scene wherever it may be. Describe it in your mind's eye – all the decorations, the Christmas tree, the party-like atmosphere. Everyone is happy and excited. Perhaps you helped decorate the room in question. Recall that now.

Bring to mind also who is there with you – your close friends, your neighbours, perhaps your brothers or sisters or even your parents. It does not matter who is in the scene once they are people who are close to you. Stay with this scene for a few moments.

Recall now any special moments of giving and receiving Christmas gifts. To whom are you giving presents? Name them in your mind. Who is giving you presents? Call to mind who they are.

Life itself is the greatest and most precious gift we have. As we sit in silence we give thanks to God for the breath of life, for the very breath that we breathe now. Once again become aware of your breath and how gently you are breathing. You did not ask for this breath, but you received it as a precious gift from God our creator. Stay with your breath. As you breathe in say in your mind 'I give thanks for the gift of life.' As you breathe out, name each person who is very special to you this Christmas time.

Conclusion

Either of the ones given on p. 15 or one of the leader's choice

Meditation 12: Advent 4

Introduction

Either of those given on pp. 12, 13 and 14 or one
of the leader's choice

Meditation/Fantasy

In your mind's eye, picture if you can the day your newly born
sister or brother was brought home from the hospital. Perhaps
it's your newly born niece or nephew or even the child of a
friend. Picture the excitement on the faces of the mother, the
father, brothers and sisters, uncles and aunts.

Birth is a special time, a precious time, a time of new life, hope
and future expectation. Imagine yourself picking up the baby and
cradling him or her in your arms. Describe this tiny life as vividly
as you can – the colour of the eyes, the tiny nose, the delicate
little fingers and nails and the colour of his or her hair. Innocent,
precious, gentle and tender – these are the new beginnings of
life.

Imagine now that you are back in your home just after you
yourself were born. See your mother and father picking you up
and cradling you in their arms. Try to remain with this image for
a few moments now.

In these last few days as we approach Christmas; we are preparing to welcome the Child Jesus into the world, innocent and tender, the Prince of Peace. Christmas is a time for Peace, a time for Hope, a time for the promise of new life.

Gently now return to an awareness of your breathing. As you breathe in, say in your mind: 'Welcome, Lord Jesus.' As you breathe out repeat: 'Welcome home!' Repeat this mantra several times.

Conclusion

Either of the ones given on p. 15 or one of the leader's choice

Meditation 13: Epiphany/Journey/I

Introduction

Either of those given on pp. 12, 13 and 14 or one
of the leader's choice

Meditation/Fantasy

We are now going to go on a journey of trust. It's a journey we
have all been on. It is our own journey of growing up to be the
person we are now. Try to recall the very first memory you have
of yourself. Attempt to enter that scene as vividly as you can.
Paint in all the details of that situation – where it was, whether
outside or inside the house, who was there with you and what
time of year it was. This is your first memory. Remain with that
scene for a few moments now.

Call to mind the very first holiday you went on. Where was it?
Who was there with you? Call them to mind now. What was the
weather like? Did you travel to the countryside, to the city, or
perhaps to a foreign country? Call that to mind now. Remain
with this scene for a minute or two.

Next, bring to mind the memory of your confirmation day. Paint
in the scene, the church, all the other pupils and adults
thronging around, the bishop and the priests. Call to mind the
adults who were with you. Mention them by name in your mind
one by one. Stay with this now for a moment or two. Where did
you go afterwards? Did you go to visit relatives, or even to a
restaurant for a meal? Try to capture the magic of the day.

You have been on a journey of trust. There have been grown-ups
of special significance for you who have helped you along the
way. You trusted these adults to help and support you. Bring to

mind these adults who have helped you one by one. Thank God for each of them. Life is like that – it's a journey of trust.

We are now going to go on another journey of trust. It's the journey of the Three Wise Men to visit the infant Jesus. These three Kings trusted the angels or messengers of the Lord to lead them the right way. They trusted God so much that they set out to find a little infant whom they believed was a special King, a special Prince of Peace. Imagine the scene as we slowly read the following account of their journey of trust:

Scriptural Reflection

After Jesus had been born at Bethlehem in Judaea during the reign of King Herod, some wise men came to Jerusalem from the East. 'Where is the infant King of the Jews?' they asked... And there in front of them was the star they had seen rising; it went forward and halted over the place where the child was. The sight of the star filled them with delight and going into the house they saw the child with his mother Mary, and falling to their knees they did him homage. Then, opening their treasures, they offered him gifts of gold, frankincense and myrrh. But they were warned in a dream not to go back to Herod, and they returned to their own country a different way.

MATTHEW 2:1-12, EDITED

Conclusion

Either of the ones given on p. 15 or one of the leader's choice

Meditation 14: Exam Time

Introduction

Either of those given on pp. 12, 13 and 14 or one of the leader's choice

Meditation/Fantasy

Imagine now that you are entering the exam hall. Bring to mind exactly how you feel right now. Who else is in the hall? Teachers. Other pupils. Notice all the noises of trepidation and anxiety before you start. However, today you are relaxed because you know that you have done as much study as you are capable of, or that time has allowed you. There is no need to feel panicky because that does not do you any good. All it can do is reduce your results if you get over-worried. Picture yourself in your seat reading the examination questions slowly. You are able to understand the questions. You know that you will be able to do yourself justice. You are taking nice slow breaths and are going to do the questions in a certain order, taking the easiest one first and then the next easiest and so on. You know you will get on just fine in this exam.

Nice and slowly now, put yourself in the following New Testament scene. You are walking along in early Palestine probably through a sandy region and you are with the disciples following Jesus:

Scriptural Reflection

Then Jesus said to his disciples, 'And so I tell you not to worry about the food you need to stay alive or about the clothes you need for your body. Life is much more important than food, and the body much more important than clothes. Look at the crows: they don't sow seeds or gather a harvest; they don't have storerooms or barns; God feeds them! You are worth so much more than birds! Can any of you live a bit longer by worrying about it? If you can't manage even such a small thing, why worry about the other things? Look how the wild flowers grow: they don't work or make clothes for themselves. But I tell you that not even King Solomon with all his wealth had clothes as beautiful as any one of these flowers. It is God who clothes the wild grass – grass that is here today and gone tomorrow, burnt up in the oven. Won't he be all the more sure to clothe you? How little faith you have! So don't be all upset, always concerned about what you will eat and drink. Your Father knows that you need these things. Instead be concerned with his Kingdom, and he will provide you with all these things.

LUKE 12:22-31

Conclusion

Either of the ones given on p. 15 or one of the leader's choice

Meditation 15: Wet, Gloomy Day

Introduction

Either of those given on pp. 12, 13 and 14 or one of the leader's choice

Meditation/Fantasy

Imagine for a moment a parched, dry land. The clay is baked hard on the ground. All the grass is burnt yellow. It is hot and stifling and the sun is blazing down. Your mouth is dry and you are dripping with sweat. How you long not alone for a drink of water, but for rain to come to soften the land, to bring back life to the soil and green growth to the grass.

Imagine now that the rain clouds are coming, that it is beginning to rain. Feel the first drops as they wet your head. See the rain seeping through the soil. You can almost feel the relief of the clay as the raindrops soften it. See the burnt, yellow grass begin to come to life again, begin to grow and become green and fresh with new life. See the rivers begin to fill up and flow, bountiful with life, with fish of all kinds.

We take the rain too much for granted. It is such a good and refreshing thing. It keeps us alive and healthy by providing us with water to drink, to keep our power plants alive with electricity, to keep our factories going. We can enjoy the rain if we really change our outlook. A rainy day need not be a gloomy day. A rainy day can be such a good and enjoyable day. Once again, feel the raindrops on your head and give thanks for the life they shower us with.

Scriptural Reflection

God said: 'Let there be a vault in the waters to divide the waters in two.' And so it was. God made the vault, and it divided the waters above the vault from the waters under the vault. God called the vault Heaven. God said: 'Let the waters under heaven come together into a single mass, and let dry land appear.' And so it was. God called the dry land 'earth' and the mass of waters 'seas', and God saw that it was good.

GENESIS 1:6-10

Conclusion

Either of the ones given on p. 15 or one of the leader's choice

Meditation 16: Winter

Introduction

Either of those given on pp. 12, 13 and 14 or one
of the leader's choice

Meditation/Fantasy

As winter draws in, the days become shorter and the nights
darker. We go to work and school under the cover of darkness.
Winter is a time when nature goes to sleep. The trees are bare;
their once lush branches are now naked limbs. The grass has
stopped growing and many animals have gone into hibernation
to sleep the cold winter away.

Call to mind now all the things you associate with winter: the
shorter days and the longer nights, the cold and the dark, the
lights crystal clear in the frosty air. Now and again we wake to
the sudden fall of a blanket of snow, which brightens a dark
winter. Recall a time when the snow fell. Picture the scene. It is
like a Christmas card. There is a beauty and purity in its brilliant
whiteness. See yourself and your friends playing in the snow,
throwing snowballs, tobogganing down the hills, or the little
children making snowmen. All is calm, beautiful and gentle just
like the mysterious silence of the fall of the snowflakes
themselves. Try to capture now that calmness and silence. Notice
how slow things become. The cars all travel more slowly and
people walk with more care.

Imagine now the taste of the snow as it melts on your lips, the
freezing cold of the snow against your hands as you make a
snowball.

We need these winter times to take stock of things, to reflect on where we are going in life. We need to slow down and enjoy the beauty of the moment. Often, a sudden snowfall allows us to do that, to slow down, take things easy, reflect on life, stop rushing about and live in the now.

Scriptural Reflection

All you works of the Lord, O bless the Lord.
To him be highest glory and praise for ever.

And you, showers and dew, o bless the Lord.
And you, frosts and cold, o bless the Lord.
And you, frost and snow, o bless the Lord.
To him be highest glory and praise for ever.

FROM 'THE CANTICLE OF DANIEL'

Conclusion

Either of the ones given on p. 15 or one of the leader's choice

Meditation 17: In the Eye of the S

Introduction

Either of those given on pp. 12, 13 and 14 or one
of the leader's choice

Meditation/Fantasy

From time to time we find ourselves in a situation that calls on all
our reserves. It may be an illness in the family, indeed an illness
you suffer from yourself. Or it may be the death of a loved one.
Maybe it's a financial crisis or a problem with bullying at work or
school. This crisis situation can be anything that really turns our
life upside-down on us for a short or even an extended period of
time. Whatever this crisis may be that you choose to bring to
mind now, it may be big or small, but for you it is a major and
important one because it is upsetting your day-to-day
functioning at work or school. You may feel like you are in the
eye of a storm.

Imagine now that you are back in Biblical times. Imagine that
you are back at the time of Jesus in Palestine. In fact you are
among his disciples, walking by the Sea of Galilee. You are one of
the disciples following along the way of The Lord. The sea is calm
and blue. There is only a very gentle breeze blowing and it is still
warm, as the sun has not yet set. There are boats left here and
there along the strand. Fishermen are mending their nets.

m

Scriptural Reflection

On the evening of that same day Jesus said to his disciples, 'Let us go across to the other side of the lake.' So they left the crowd; the disciples got into the boat in which Jesus was already sitting, and they took him with them. Other boats were there too. Suddenly a strong wind blew up, and the waves began to spill over into the boat, so that it was about to fill with water. Jesus was in the back of the boat, sleeping with his head on a pillow. The disciples woke him up and said, 'Teacher, don't you care that we are about to drown?'

Jesus stood up and commanded the wind, 'Be quiet!' And he said to the waves, 'Be still!' The wind died down, and there was a great calm. Then Jesus said to his disciples, 'Why are you so frightened? Have you still no faith?' But they were terribly afraid and said to one another, 'Who is this man? Even the wind and waves obey him!'

MARK 4:35-41

Conclusion

Either of the ones given on p. 15 or one of the leader's choice

Meditation 18: Doubt

Introduction

Either of those given on pp. 12, 13 and 14 or one
of the leader's choice

Meditation/Fantasy

It's so easy to be cynical, that is, to doubt the motives of others.
When was the last time you said of someone 'Aw, he's only in it
for what he can get out of it.' or 'She's only doing it to lick up to
the boss.' Try to bring to mind now any instance when you have
doubted the motives of another person.

Did anyone ever promise to do something for you and fail to
fulfil that undertaking? Bring that situation and that person to
mind. Ask yourself, 'Did I end up doubting the promises of others
as a result? Do I really trust others?'

When was the last time I promised to do something and failed to
deliver? Bring that situation to mind. Whom did I hurt? Do others
doubt me as a result? Do others really trust me?

It's so easy to be negative, so much harder to be positive. When
I'm positive I have to trust others, trust myself; trust in the basic
goodness of life. If often means living on risk... But risk is worth
it, worth the trust because all too often we will be surprised at
the goodness of others.

Cast your mind back to the first time you learned to cycle or to
swim or to drive. You never doubted that you would do it, did
you? Who was there to teach you or encourage you? They did
not doubt you, because if they did you probably would have
given up.

It's so easy to doubt ourselves, to doubt others and, indeed, to doubt our faith. Doubt, too, often is the easy way out. It's always so much harder to have faith, to trust that others won't let us down, to take the leap in the dark, to reach out for the hand that will pull us to safety.

Scriptural Reflection

The Apostles said to the Lord, 'Make our faith greater.' The Lord answered, 'If you had faith as big as a mustard seed, you could say to this mulberry tree, "Pull yourself up by the roots and plant yourself in the sea!" and it would obey you.'

LUKE 17:5-6

Conclusion

Either of the ones given on p. 15 or one of the leader's choice

Meditation 19: Forgiveness

Introduction

Either of those given on pp. 12, 13 and 14 or one
of the leader's choice

Meditation/Fantasy

Think of the last time that you had a disagreement or row with
somebody. Try to recapture what that experience was like. Bring
the person to mind. Picture the situation, where you both were.
Relive the argument or disagreement in your imagination. What
was it about? What were you feeling?

What was it like to walk away hurt? Perhaps you later made up
with that person or perhaps you didn't. In either event, imagine
now that you are about to make up with that person, to re-unite
what has been broken as best you can. How are you feeling as
you approach each other? Who is going to make the first move?
Is it you or the other person? Sense how difficult it is to do so.
Yet it is definitely worth the effort. Picture the scene in detail as
you say 'sorry' for the misunderstanding, or indeed for the deep
hurt you both have inflicted on each other.

Growth is always painful. It's never easy. We learn by our mistakes.
We can learn a lot from mutual hurts if we really try to reach out.
To reach out in forgiveness. To try to re-unite the bond that has
been broken. Making up is always hard to do, but it is always
worth the effort. When we do so, we learn a lot about ourselves
and a lot about the other people involved. Another question worth
asking ourselves is: 'Can I forgive myself? Can I forgive myself even
when everyone else has forgiven me?' It's important also to be
gentle with ourselves, to be able to forgive ourselves, to take Jesus
at his word that our sins are forgiven when he has told us so.

Scriptural Reflection

Jesus is speaking to us now in the words of Luke's Gospel:
I tell you: whenever you pray and ask for something, believe that you have received it, and you will be given whatever you ask for. And when you stand and pray, forgive anything you may have against anyone, so that your Father in heaven will forgive the wrongs you have done.

LUKE 11:2-5

Conclusion

Either of the ones given on p. 15 or one of the leader's choice

Meditation 20: Healing

Introduction

Either of those given on pp. 12, 13 and 14 or one
of the leader's choice

Meditation/Fantasy

Cast your mind back to the last time you were sick. You may
have had the flu or a sprained ankle or a bad bout of asthma. Try
to recapture the experience for a few moments. Where are you –
at home, perhaps in bed? Try to picture the scene now in your
mind's eye.

Imagine a healing light or heat playing over the infected or
injured area. If you had the flu imagine how the heat of that light
burns away the fever. If you had a sprained ankle or a torn
ligament imagine that heat healing the muscles or ligaments,
repairing what was torn. If you suffered from an asthma attack
imagine that light playing on your chest and nasal regions,
unblocking all your breathing passages.

Become aware of your breathing. Notice how your chest rises
and falls ever so gently with each breath you take. Feel its rise
and fall for a few moments. With each breath you take, the very
breath of life is healing you. As you breathe in and out say with
each breath you take the words 'breath of life' over and over for
a few moments.

Scriptural Reflection

When Jesus came down from the hill, large crowds followed him.
Then a man suffering from a dreaded skin disease came to him,
knelt down before him, and said, 'Sir, if you want to you can
make me clean.' Jesus stretched out his hand and touched him. 'I
do want to,' he answered. 'Be clean!' At once the man was
healed of his disease. Then Jesus said to him, 'Listen! Don't tell
anyone, but go straight to the priest and let him examine you;
then in order to prove to everyone that you are cured, offer the
sacrifice that Moses ordered.'

MATTHEW 8:1-4

Conclusion

Either of the ones given on p. 15 or one of the leader's choice

Meditation 21: Journey

Introduction

Either of those given on pp. 12, 13 and 14 or one
of the leader's choice

Meditation/Fantasy

There are many times in our lives when we set out on a journey. Holiday times especially, but there are also other times when we set out to go to a special function like a wedding, a concert, a party, a baptism or even a funeral. Perhaps we are setting out to see a friend or relative whom we haven't seen for years. In another and more important sense we can say that life itself is a journey, a rather unique one from birth to death.

In this meditation I want you to imagine that you are setting out on a journey by train. Imagine now the preparations you make for that trip. Call to mind also how the train station looks. Try to enter the atmosphere of a busy city station. Hear the noises as trains come in and leave, the sounds of doors opening and shutting, the messages over the intercom. Who are you with at the station? To whom are you saying goodbye? Capture the scene. Are you happy or sad at this departure? Are you full of expectation for what may lie ahead?

See yourself purchasing your ticket. It is time now to get on the train. Imagine what that's like as you take your seat. Look out through the window. Once again notice the sounds and movements as the train begins to set off. Notice the gradually quickening scenes through the windows until finally all becomes a blur.

Where are you going on this journey? Only you know your destination. In your own mind now imagine your very own destination. As you sit in your carriage seat you close your eyes and bring your place of destination to mind. Your heart is full of expectation for the place where you are going. Who will be there to meet you?

Imagine now that you have finally arrived. Once again bring all the sounds and scenes of your destination to mind. It may be a small country train station or even a large city one. You are grabbing your luggage. There is a crush of people waiting to descend onto the platform. Who is there to greet you? You see that person now through the glass of the window. He or she is smiling and is delighted to see you. Imagine now getting off the train and your mutual delight at seeing each other. Imagine you both embracing.

Conclusion

Either of the ones given on p. 15 or one of the leader's choice

Meditation 22: Spring

Introduction

Either of those given on pp. 12, 13 and 14 or one of the leader's choice

Meditation/Fantasy

Imagine that you are in your favourite outdoor place, in the country, on top of a hill or mountain, walking by a river or stream, on a beach or walking by the coast. Wherever your favourite outdoor place may be, paint it in your mind with all its qualities. The time of day. The sun shining brightly in the sky. It is this time of year, late February, and spring is beginning to blossom around you. Notice the first buds of leaves on the trees. The first snowdrops dangling their fragile heads in the sun. The first signs of the stalks of daffodils or tulips stabbing through the black clay. Along the hedgerows the yellow primroses are all blossoming brilliantly. The air is pure and fresh, though still with a spring chill. So wherever your favourite outdoor place is, describe it in your mind. The clouds, the colour of the hills or mountains, the colour of the water in the river or sea. Is there anyone else around? Are there any animals nearby? Notice whatever birds there may be in the branches of the trees, on the grass or wading along the seashore. Notice how peaceful everything is around you. Notice how peaceful and relaxed you are as you walk along.

Now choose a spot in your favourite outdoor space and sit down. You are indeed truly relaxed. Listen to the music of the birds as they sing about you, the gentle lapping of the water as it rolls past you. You are breathing in the new life of spring. Nature is beginning to come alive after the sleepy, dormant months of winter. Its new life is beginning to refresh your spirit. You are

becoming more and more enlivened and energised as you breathe in the fresh air of spring. Gently become aware of your breathing. Notice the colder air as you breathe in and the warmer air as you breathe out. As you breathe in, welcome the Lord of Life, the God who breathes his sustaining breath into each of us and keeps us alive. As you breathe in say in your mind 'Welcome, Lord of Life'. As you breathe out say with each breath 'Welcome, Lord of Spring'. Gently continue this mantra for a few minutes.

Conclusion

Either of the ones given on p. 15 or one of the leader's choice

Meditation 23: Desert (Lent 1)

Introduction

Either of those given on pp. 12, 13 and 14 or one
of the leader's choice

Meditation/Fantasy

Imagine now for a minute that you are out training, or that you
are coming near the end of a long run. You are quite exhausted
and very thirsty. Your mouth is dry. How you long for a nice drink
of refreshing water and for a shower. Now imagine that you are a
traveller in a desert. The sun is beating down on you. Your face,
which is exposed to the sun, is burnt. Your tongue is dry. You
have very little water left and you know you have miles to go
before you reach the only oasis where you can refill your flask.
Feel what this struggle is like, the dryness of your mouth, your
lack of energy, the scalding heat, the irritating sand and the pain
in your eyes from the sun.

Life is like that sometimes. Sometimes we have to travel through
our very own deserts. These may be times when some relative
gets sick or dies, or when we ourselves are low or depressed. Call
to mind any time that you were not feeling well. Call to mind
your own personal desert.

Bring your mind back now to the actual desert. See yourself
finally arriving at a beautiful oasis. Picture that scene now in your
mind's eye. See the lush palm trees around a beautiful well. See
yourself crawling – with your last ounce of energy – over to the
side of that well. Feel and taste the cool water as it washes over
your dry tongue and quenches your thirst.

You may have experienced a desert in your own life, a time
when you felt alone, deserted and without much comfort.
Where was the oasis for you in your own desert? Was there

someone special there who helped you? Give thanks for that person. Give thanks for their help and care.

Scriptural Reflection

Filled with the Holy Spirit, Jesus left the Jordan and was led by the Spirit through the wilderness, being tempted there by the devil for forty days. During that time he ate nothing and at the end he was hungry. Then the devil said to him, 'If you are the Son of God, tell this stone to turn into a loaf.' But Jesus replied, 'Scripture says: Man does not live on bread alone.'

Then leading him to a height, the devil showed him in a moment of time all the kingdoms of the world and said to him, 'I will give you all this power and the glory of all these kingdoms, for it has been committed to me and I give it to anyone I choose.' But Jesus said to him, 'Scripture says you must worship the Lord your God, and serve him alone.'

Then he led him to Jerusalem and made him stand on the parapet of the Temple. 'If you are the Son of God,' he said to him, 'throw yourself down from here and the angels will save you.' But Jesus answered him, 'You must not put the Lord your God to the test.'

Having exhausted all these ways of tempting him, the devil left him, to return at the appointed time.

LUKE 4:1-13

Conclusion

Either of the ones given on p. 15 or one of the leader's choice

Meditation 24: Our Desire for God

Introduction

Either of those given on pp. 12, 13 and 14 or one
of the leader's choice

Meditation/Fantasy

Think for a moment of any thing or things you have desired
throughout your life. Perhaps it was the latest fashionable
mountain-bike, computer or clothes. Bring that thing to mind
now. Perhaps you had to save up for it. Now remember the time
you got that object. Picture your delight.

Now recall weeks or months after you have acquired this article.
Notice how you began to take it for granted, how you began to
treat it more casually and with less care. This happens with all
worldly things. At first they delight us, but gradually their
attraction begins to dim. We always want more!

Often it is the same in relationships with our families and friends.
In any relationship there is a honeymoon period where
everything seems golden, but gradually we realise that we are
capable of hurting each other, and hopefully of forgiving each
other. Bring any relationship to mind now. What hurts have you
both suffered in this friendship? Gradually we realise that real life
is never a honeymoon, and that even our relationships reach
some sort of plateau and are very hard work.

Deep within every one of us there is a deep hunger for
fulfilment. Our deepest hunger is for God. There is a basic
loneliness at the heart of every human being, which can be filled
by God alone. We are never totally content or happy on this
earth, whether in our possessions or in our relationships. We all

have our own particular questions in our hearts, questions that we may find hard to resolve. What are the questions that arise for you at this moment?

Scriptural Reflection

Jesus took with him Peter and John and James and went up the mountains to pray. As he prayed the aspect of his face was changed and his clothing became brilliant as lightning. Suddenly there were two men there talking to him; they were Moses and Elijah appearing in glory, and they were speaking of his passing which was to come in Jerusalem. Peter and his companions were heavy with sleep, but they kept awake and saw his glory and the two men standing with him. As these were leaving him, Peter said to Jesus, 'Master, it is wonderful for us to be here; so let us make three tents, one for you, one for Moses and one for Elijah.' – He did not know what he was saying. As he spoke, a cloud came and covered them with shadow; and when they went into the cloud the disciples were afraid. And a voice came from the cloud saying, 'This is my Son, the Chosen One. Listen to him.' And after the voice had spoken, Jesus was found alone. The disciples kept silent and, at that time, told no one what they had seen.

LUKE 9:28-36

Conclusion

Either of the ones given on p. 15 or one of the leader's choice

Meditation 25: Repentance (Lent

Introduction

Either of those given on pp. 12, 13 and 14 or one
of the leader's choice

Meditation/Fantasy

Every worthwhile job we do requires preparation. If we set out to
plant shrubs and flowers in our garden the soil will need a lot of
preparation. If we have to paint anything we must first clean and
prepare the surface. Recall the last time you did some repairs or
decoration around the house, the garden or the school. What
were the preparations you made? Put yourself back in that scene.
Perhaps you were helping someone strip wallpaper. Or perhaps
you were sanding a door or a wooden floor so that it could be
varnished. Whatever your job was, bring that particular task to
mind now. Recall all the preparations you made on the day in
question. All these were necessary for the job to be done well.

One such preparation I need in the spiritual life so that I will
grow is called repentance, or turning away from my sinful past or
from sinful aspects of my personality… To be made ready to
enter the Kingdom of God, I must first repent… I must change
my direction in life. Lent is a great time to take stock, to look at
my direction in life… What is the yardstick by which I guide my
life? Am I selfish? Am I intolerant of individuals or groups? Am I
lazy or self-indulgent? Do I do an honest day's work for an honest
day's pay?

Scriptural Reflection

Jesus told this parable: 'A man had a fig tree in his vineyard, and he came looking for fruit on it but he found none. He said to the man who looked after the vineyard, "Look here, for three years now I have been coming looking for fruit on this fig tree and finding none. Cut it down: why should it be taking up the ground?" "Sir," replied the man, "leave it one more year and give me time to dig round it and manure it: it may bear fruit next year; if not, then you can cut it down."'

LUKE 13:6-9

Conclusion

Either of the ones given on p. 15 or one of the leader's choice

Meditation 26: Trust (Lent 4)

Introduction

Either of those given on pp. 12, 13 and 14 or one
of the leader's choice

Meditation/Fantasy

We all get into tricky situations or tight corners at some stage in
our lives. Sometimes the situation seems to be hopeless or
pointless. Perhaps it is because we have done very little study for
our exams, or have done very little training and have been
dropped from the team, or have broken our leg and are
depressed. Perhaps you have been caught doing something
wrong and feel really ashamed. Maybe you feel you have let
someone special down. Whatever the reason, sometimes the
bottom seems to fall out of our world.

Recall a time when it seemed that there was no hope for you –
when the bottom dropped out of your world. Bring that situation
to mind. What happened? What were the consequences for you?
Who were the people who challenged you or who were getting
at you? Was there any person who offered hope in your
situation? Was there any one person whom you trusted? If there
was bring that person to mind now. Or perhaps there was some
important step that you took yourself – like saying sorry or asking
for forgiveness. To trust that the other person will accept our
apology takes huge courage. But it is worth it. A seemingly
unresolved and difficult problem can seem like a long dark
tunnel. Imagine that tunnel now in your mind's eye, how black
and hopeless it is. Now see yourself eventually coming out of that
tunnel and into the light.

In our observance of Lent we must never lose sight of our goal which is Easter Sunday and the glory of the resurrection. With this in mind we can really trust in Christ who is our light along the dark path of Lent and life.

Scriptural Reflection

When he had finished speaking he said to Simon, 'Put out into the deep water and pay out your nets for a catch.' 'Master,' Simon replied, 'we worked hard all night long and caught nothing, but if you say so, I will pay out the nets.' And when they had done this they netted such a huge number of fish that their nets began to tear, so they signalled to their companions in the other boats to come and help them; when these came, they filled the two boats to sinking point.

Luke 5:4-11

Conclusion

Either of the ones given on p. 15 or one of the leader's choice

Meditation 27: Meal/Eucharist/Ho

Introduction

Either of those given on pp. 12, 13 and 14 or one
of the leader's choice

Meditation/Fantasy

Recall now the last time you had a meal with people that you
love. Call that situation vividly to mind. It is a special occasion.
Those who are present are close and beloved to you. What are
you celebrating? Is it a birthday or an anniversary? Is it a special
occasion like Christmas or Easter? Or is it to celebrate the return
home of a brother or sister or friend who has been away a long
time? Whatever the occasion may be visualise now one by one
everyone who is present.

Meals are special times of sharing, special times of celebration,
occasions when we know we belong to one another in a very
special way. Picture the last time you may have had a meal with
your friends. Notice how relaxed you all are, how much part of
each other you all feel – how you belong.

When people are going away for an extended period of time
they often like to have a meal with their family and friends. This
is a special time and it says a lot, which words simply can't. Try
to recapture, if you can, the feeling of togetherness and support
at such a meal.

When Jesus knew that he was going away, that he was physically
leaving his Apostles, he desired very much to have a last meal
with his chosen twelve, his twelve special friends. That meal
became something wonderful for all Christians because at that
meal Jesus left them a very special gift called the Eucharist, which

they could share with his true followers everywhere. That Last Supper was the first celebration of Mass, as we know it. When we celebrate the Eucharist we enter into a very special relationship or fellowship with the Risen Lord. Jesus told his disciples that he would be always with them in a special way wherever bread was broken in his name, whenever they did so 'in memory' of him.

Scriptural Reflection

When they drew near to the village, he (the unrecognised Jesus) made as if to go on, but they pressed him to stay with them. 'It is nearly evening,' they said, 'and the day is almost over.' So he went in to stay with them. Now while he was with them at table, he took the bread and said the blessing; then he broke it and handed it to them. And their eyes were opened and they recognised him; but he had vanished from their sight. Then they said to each other: 'Did not our hearts burn within us as he talked to us on the road and explained the Scriptures to us?'

LUKE 24: 13-35
(SHORTENED VERSION — IF THE LEADER SO WISHES
HE/SHE MIGHT LIKE TO USE THE FULL VERSION)

Conclusion

Either of the ones given on p. 15 or one of the leader's choice

Meditation 28: Suffering/Passion/(

Introduction

Either of those given on pp. 12, 13 and 14 or one
of the leader's choice

Meditation/Fantasy

Call to mind someone whom you know well and who has
suffered a lot. Perhaps it's a member of your family, or a good
friend, or a neighbour. Briefly try to enter into what that suffering
must be like for that person. It may be very difficult to imagine,
but it's worth trying and may help us to empathise with them.
What are all the things that person can't do? Try to imagine the
efforts that person has to make just to do the simple things that
you take for granted.

Imagine for a moment that you have broken your leg. Go
through all the things you would have to do to get up in the
morning just to perform the normal everyday things like dressing
and making your way to the kitchen to have your breakfast.
Imagine for just a few minutes how you would manage doing
just these few things.

Suffering comes to us all. Our power and control over our lives
are taken away. We are left depending on the goodness of
others. We find it hard to go on. We hate being dependent on
others. We miss our freedom. We cry out in pain, in annoyance,
in anger. Why did God allow this to happen to me? Why me,
Lord? Why me?

d Friday

Imagine now for a moment that you are one of the crowds along the route of Our Lord's Passion that first Good Friday. See Jesus carrying his cross. See him struggling with the cross. See him falling to the ground under its great weight. See Simon of Cyrene helping him. See the pain on his face, the crown of thorns on his head, and the blood caked across his forehead and the sweat trickling down. Hear his groans of pain.

Scriptural Reflection

They brought Jesus to the place called Golgotha, which means the place of the skull. They offered him wine mixed with myrrh, but he refused it. Then they crucified him and shared out his clothing, casting lots to decide what each should get. The inscription giving the charge against him read: 'The King of the Jews.' And they crucified two robbers with him, one on his right and one on his left.'

MARK 15:22-27

Conclusion

Either of the ones given on p. 15 or one of the leader's choice

Meditation 29: New Life/Resurrect

Introduction

Either of those given on pp. 12, 13 and 14 or one
of the leader's choice

Meditation/Fantasy

Imagine for a moment a scene from nature. See a caterpillar on a
green leaf eating it away. But the time comes when the
caterpillar must die, when it shrivels up and becomes a chrysalis,
and from that a beautiful butterfly eventually emerges. Imagine
now for a moment or two this process of death, transformation
and new life.

Or again, imagine a man or woman going out to plant some
seeds in the fertile ground. See the seeds falling. Focus on one
such seed and see it in its dark, clay bed. There is no light. All is
dark and smothering. The seed is dry and practically lifeless, but
the water comes to give it new life. Eventually small, delicate
roots push their way out, down out through the ruptured shell of
the seed, and delicate stems push their green, tender shoots up
through the clay to meet the light of the invigorating day. Death,
transformation and new life again.

Easter Sunday

Scriptural Reflection

It is the same with the resurrection of the dead: the thing that is sown is perishable, but what is raised is imperishable. The thing that is sown is contemptible, but what is raised is glorious; the thing that is sown is weak, but what is raised is powerful; when it is sown it embodies the soul, when it is raised it embodies the spirit... I will tell you something that has been a secret: that we are not all going to die, but we shall all be changed. This will be instantaneous, in the twinkling of an eye, when the last trumpet sounds. It will sound, and the dead will be raised, imperishable, and we shall be changed as well, because our present perishable nature must put on imperishability and this mortal nature must put on immortality.

1 Corinthians 15:42-53

Conclusion

Either of the ones given on p. 15 or one of the leader's choice

Meditation 30: Light

Introduction

Either of those given on pp. 12, 13 and 14 or one
of the leader's choice

Meditation/Fantasy

Imagine now that you are walking outdoors, somewhere in a
country or nature setting. Paint this scene in your mind's eye. It is
a beautiful day. There are very few clouds, if any, in the sky. There
is a mild, gentle breeze blowing through your hair. You are really
happy in yourself, as are all the other people whom you may
meet or see today. It is a day that is full of life and light. This
morning when you awoke you noticed the sun poking long,
bright fingers of light through the gaps in the blinds. It was so
bright outside that the thought of remaining in bed was
unattractive. The light of the sun was too attractive to be
ignored. All of nature, not just human beings, responds to the
positive and invigorating energy of the sun. The grass, the leaves
and the stems of plants all grow towards its life-giving warmth.

Today you are walking in the sun, walking in the light. The sun
itself is a source of life in our own solar system. This strong light
of the sun, as you walk slowly and peacefully, sustains you now.
Imagine yourself lying down on the side of a green hill and the
sun shining on your face. You are very relaxed and very peaceful.

Again, imagine yourself on a hill, but this time you are sitting
down with a lot of other people and you are listening to Jesus
preach – this is what he is saying to all who are gathered to listen
to him:

Scriptural Reflection

This life brought light to mankind. The light shines in the darkness, and the darkness has never put it out…

ADAPTED FROM JOHN 1

You are like light for the whole world. A city build on a hill cannot be hidden. No one lights a lamp and puts it under a bowl; instead he puts it on the lamp stand, where it gives light for everyone in the house. In the same way your light must shine before people, so they will see the good things you do and praise your Father in heaven.

MATTHEW 5: 14-16

Conclusion

Either of the ones given on p. 15 or one of the leader's choice

Meditation 31: Water

Introduction

Either of those given on pp. 12, 13 and 14 or one
of the leader's choice

Meditation/Fantasy

Imagine now that you are out in the country on a hike or a long
walk. You are walking along a country path with bushes and trees
on both sides. In the distance you can see the mountains with
their steep green and blue sides. Become part of this scene.
Imagine yourself walking along. Your friends accompany you. Call
each one of them to mind and name each one. Finally the path
leads out into an open space and wide green fields lie open
before you. In the distance you can still see the mountains, but
this time you can also notice clearly the white track of a waterfall
on the lower right hand side of the mountain.

You and your friends are going to go there. You are going to go
right over there and picnic at its edge. Bit by bit, the waterfall is
becoming clearer to the eye. Gradually as you journey along you
are beginning to hear the water hissing gently. As you approach
ever closer to this waterfall, it gets bigger and bigger and the
rushing sounds of the water become louder and louder until they
make a crashing sound. Hear these crashing sounds now in your
imagination. Notice how brilliantly clear the water is, how white
it is when it crashes over the sharp edges of the rocks and when
it hits the bottom of the fall. Imagine now that you can stand
beneath the waterfall. With some difficulty, you clamber over the
great rocks and go in under them. It is slippery on the outside,
but finally you find a fairly dry spot and sit down. You decide to
close your eyes and listen to the water crash and thunder down.

Scriptural Reflection

There was a Jewish leader named Nicodemus, who belonged to the party of the Pharisees. One night he went to Jesus and said to him, 'Rabbi, we know that you are a teacher sent by God. No one could perform the miracles you are doing unless God were with him.' Jesus answered, 'I am telling you the truth: no one can see the Kingdom of God unless he is born again.'

'How can a grown man be born again?' Nicodemus asked. 'He certainly cannot enter his mother's womb and be born a second time!' 'I am telling you the truth,' replied Jesus. 'No one can enter the Kingdom of God unless he is born of water and the Spirit.'

JOHN 3:1-5

Conclusion

Either of the ones given on p. 15 or one of the leader's choice

Meditation 32: Summer

Introduction

Either of those given on pp. 12, 13 and 14 or one
of the leader's choice

Meditation/Fantasy

Imagine now that you are on your holidays by the sea. Picture it
in your mind. It is a beautiful day. The sea is calm and blue; the
sand golden-brown and warm underfoot. See if you can sense
the feel of the warm sand between your toes as you walk on it

Who else is on the beach? Which of your friends are there? Name
them. There is not a cloud in the sky and the sun is shining
brilliantly. Now imagine running into the water. It is cold at first.
Notice the stones and shells as they bruise the soles of your feet
as you venture further out. Now the water is waist-high. Get the
feel of it. Finally it is time for the plunge into the invigorating
water. Feel the shock of its coldness as you dive into its embrace.
Sense the water in your ears and nose as you begin to cut the
waves with the strokes of your arms. Feel the air rushing up your
nostrils as you turn your head to breathe, and then experience
blowing that air out under the water.

You are now lying on your back floating. You can feel your heart
beat in your ears as you lie there calmly in the water.

Reflection/Prayer

For all the good things in life we are truly grateful. For the joy of using our senses we give thanks to the Lord of life. For the sense of touch. For the sense of smell. For the gift of sight. For the gift of hearing. For the sense of taste, like salt water on the tongue. For the gift of sampling all the delights of the senses we thank you Lord, for you created all things.

Conclusion

Either of the ones given on p. 15 or one of the leader's choice

Meditation 33: Earth (Clay)

Introduction

Either of those given on pp. 12, 13 and 14 or one of the leader's choice

Meditation/Fantasy

Imagine now that you are out in the garden. You are about to weed the border alongside the wall. It is early spring. Picture the tools you have: a small trowel or hoe. The soil is caked hard at the moment, so you have to loosen it with the hoe. As the clay is broken it takes on a new life – it begins to come alive. You notice the worms wriggling through the clay. As you weed you can hear the weeds as they are ripped from the soil. You now have clay on your hands and under your nails. Try to get that feeling now.

Clay is necessary to life – all the plants we need to eat for our well-being spring from the earth. All the trees, bushes and flowers that colour our country with wonderful variety and colour need the clay for rooting and survival. Call to mind now all the plants and trees and flowers that you see from day to day.

Think of the times that you have played football or hurling or camogie or some other game on the rich green grass of a park. Imagine now that the game is over and that you are lying back on the grass. You can smell the grass and clay in your nostrils. You can feel both the grass and the clay under you. Let your fingers run through the blades of grass and feel the soil under your nails.

Scriptural Reflection

Yahweh God fashioned man from the dust of the soil. Then he breathed into his nostrils a breath of life, and thus man became a living being. So from the soil Yahweh God fashioned all the wild beasts and all the birds of heaven.

GENESIS 2:7, 19

Conclusion

Either of the ones given on p. 15 or one of the leader's choice

Meditation 34: Air (Spirit)

Introduction

Either of those given on pp. 12, 13 and 14 or one
of the leader's choice

Meditation/Fantasy

Imagine now that you are out for a walk in the countryside. You
are on a hike. In front of you there is a fine big hill. You begin to
climb it. Notice all the bushes, trees and plants that surround
you. Become aware of the countryside as you begin to ascend
the hill. Finally you reach the top. You sit down on a rock and
you look out on the sea that is one side of you and the fields that
are on the other side. Feel the wind or air as it blows on your
face and through your hair.

Below you see the surface of the sea. It is a brilliant blue in the
sunshine. Further out you see a yacht tacking across the bay. You
see its bright, white sails billowing in the wind. Get a sense of
that now – a yacht moving across the waves, moving gently up
and down with the wind billowing in its full white sails. There are
seagulls in the sky and they are gliding through the air. Become
aware of that now – the seagulls gliding through the air.

To your right there is a big building on the hill. You look more
closely at it and you find that it is a windmill. You see a big,
huge, strong building with four great sails. Become aware of that
movement now. The power of the wind is used to move its great
sails; the sails move the machinery inside, which can grind grain
into flour.

We give thanks for the wind, which blows fresh air our way, which blows the clouds to bring us rain, which transforms itself into energy that we can use to power our houses and places of work, which allows us to enjoy such sports as sailing, windsurfing and hang-gliding.

Scriptural Reflection

When Pentecost Day came round, they all met in one room, when suddenly they heard what sounded like a powerful wind from heaven. And something appeared to them like tongues of fire… They were all filled with the Holy Spirit and began to speak foreign languages as the Spirit gave them the gift of speech.

ACTS 2:1-4

Conclusion

Either of the ones given on p. 15 or one of the leader's choice

Meditation 35: Fire

Introduction

Either of those given on pp. 12, 13 and 14 or one
of the leader's choice

Meditation/Fantasy

Imagine now that you are on a camping trip with your friends.
You are all seated around a blazing campfire. You are telling
stories, or perhaps even singing. One or two of you are tending
the fire – throwing on extra logs. See the sparks rise. Hear the
timber crack in the flames.

Once again, bring your mind back to the fire and the blazing
logs. Become aware of the flames as they consume the wood.
Become aware of their colours and shapes as they lick the air.
Feel their heat and energy. Fire is full of energy and power. When
anything burns it releases great energy that can either create or
destroy. Fire can destroy buildings and lives very rapidly. Imagine
such a scene of destruction in your mind's eye. See the flames
dance their dance of destruction in the night sky. See all the
services around the fire – fire brigades, ambulances and police
cars. Fire can also be creative as when it burns coal or turf,
creating the energy of that can be used to heat us, or can be
converted into electricity to power our houses and factories. It
provides the spark to make petrol explode, which drives our cars
and buses, ships and planes. Fire is powerful, yet destructive. We
need it to live and survive, but we need to respect it.

Scriptural Reflection

When Pentecost Day came round, they all met in one room, when suddenly they heard what sounded like a powerful wind from heaven… and something appeared to them like tongues of fire… They were all filled with the Holy Spirit and began to speak foreign languages as the Spirit gave them the gift of speech.

ACTS 2:1-4

Conclusion

Either of the ones given on p. 15 or one of the leader's choice

Meditation 36: Edmund Rice

Introduction

Either of those given on pp. 12, 13 and 14 or one
of the leader's choice

*N.B. The following meditation/fantasy can be profitably used with
any person who is inspiring for our lives as human beings trying to
follow in the way of Jesus Christ. Below, I have used Edmund Rice,
but other prophetic figures such as Martin Luther King, Mahatma
Gandhi, Mother Teresa, Nano Nagle, Pope John Paul II, Nelson
Mandela or Archbishop Desmond Tutu could easily be slotted in
instead. In short, any character of moral vision or exemplary virtue
will suffice.*

Meditation/Fantasy

Imagine now that you are in your favourite place. It can be
indoor or outdoor. Wherever it is, describe it in your mind – paint
it as vividly as you can in your imagination. If it is outside, you
see the sky, the clouds, the trees and the birds. Gently become
aware of everything around you in your favourite place. If it is
indoors, picture the room as vividly as you can in your own
mind. This place that you have chosen is your own special place
where you can go to be at your most relaxed. As you sit and
relax in this, your favourite, place become aware of how peaceful
everything is. Of how peaceful you are.

Now imagine that as you sit there someone else enters the room or comes into this place that you have chosen as your most precious space. At first, it appears to be a stranger. Then you gradually make out that it is Edmund Rice. Try to picture this man in your mind. A tall man – over six feet – with white hair, dressed in a black cloak. Notice how calm and relaxed he is. Now imagine that he begins to speak to you. What does he say? What words of encouragement would he give to you? Stay with this conversation for a few minutes.

It is now time for Edmund to go and leave you quietly relaxed in your own special place.

Conclusion

Either of the ones given on p. 15 or one of the leader's choice

Meditation 37: St Patrick

Introduction

Either of those given on pp. 12, 13 and 14 or one of the leader's choice

Meditation/Fantasy

Imagine a young man, aged sixteen, full of life, intelligence and the hopes of youth. Then imagine that you are this young man, living in 5th century Britain. Try to capture your fear as you are taken prisoner by fierce, marauding Gaels from the island of Ireland. The Romans called it 'Hibernia' – they imagined it to be a cold, wintry, forbidding place. You, too, have this feeling about Ireland. You, too, would be afraid to go there. Let your mind be filled with fear as these terrible foreigners sweep you away with many other young people – boys and girls – to the island of Hibernia. Then imagine being a slave, tending sheep and goats on a bleak mountainside. Here is Patrick in his own words from The Confession, which he wrote as an old man:

I am Patrick, a sinner, the most unlearned of men, the lowliest of all the faithful. My father was Calpornius who was a deacon and son of the priest Potitus. I was taken captive when I was about sixteen years of age. I was taken into captivity to Ireland with many thousands of people. The Lord God showed concern for my weakness, and pity for my youth and ignorance; he watched over me before I got to know him and before I was able to distinguish good from evil. In fact he protected me and comforted me as a father would a son. When I had come to Ireland I tended herds every day and I used to pray many times during the day. More and more my love for God and reverence for him began to increase. Even in times of snow or frost or rain I would rise before dawn to pray.

Try to put yourself in Patrick's position: a young boy of sixteen, frightened, yet full of faith in his God, the God of Jesus Christ in 5th century Ireland. Having escaped from Ireland to Britain at God's bidding, Patrick had the following dream:

It was there one night I saw a vision of a man called Victor, who appeared to have come from Ireland with an unlimited number of letters and he gave me one of them and I read the opening words which were; 'The voice of the Irish. We ask you, boy, come and walk once more amongst us.'

Conclusion

Either of the ones given on p. 15 or one of the leader's choice

Meditation 38: St Brigid

Introduction

Either of those given on pp. 12, 13 and 14 or one
of the leader's choice

Meditation/Fantasy

It is the beginning of spring, the 1st of February. Tentative
growth is just about to begin. The birds are beginning to gather
material for their nests; there is a promise of new light and new
life in nature. Become aware now of this promise of new growth
and life. Put yourself in some outdoor scene, somewhere in the
country. See the hills, the bare trees, which shortly will have
some little growth as evidence of spring. See the grass, the sun,
the sky, and the clouds against the blue of the distant mountains.
Spring is a time of hope and a time of promise. Feel that hope
and that promise deep within you.

Today, the 1st of February we celebrate the feast of St Brigid,
'Mary of the Gaels'.

Today we give thanks for all the good things in nature, for the
rain that keeps the land fertile, for the grass that grows lush and
feeds the herds, for the fruits and vegetables that grow so
bountifully, for the soil that nourishes them, for the frost that
breaks the clay and helps aerate it, for the fresh air we breathe
that sustains our life, for the fruits we eat from the branches and
bushes, for the milk we drink, for the flour that comes from the
grain and for the bread that we eat. For all this we are thankful.
Without the bounty of nature we would be unable to survive.

Scriptural Reflection

A sower went out to sow seed. As he sowed, some fell on the edge of the path and was trampled on; and the birds of the air ate it up. Some seed fell on rock, and when it came up it withered away, having no moisture. Some seed fell amongst thorns and the thorns grew with it and choked it. And some seed fell into rich soil and grew and produced its crop a hundredfold. Saying this Jesus cried, 'Listen anyone who has ears to hear!'

LUKE 8:5-8

Conclusion

Either of the ones given on p. 15 or one of the leader's choice

Bibliography

The following list is not exhaustive, but I have arranged it into sections that deal with meditation under its various manifestations as it appears on the bookshelves. I have also included sites worth exploring on the World-Wide Web.

A. Meditation, General Health and Psychology:

Chopra, Deepak, *Quantum Healing* (Bantam, 1989)
Chopra, Deepak, *Unconditional Life* (Bantam, 1995)
Chopra, Deepak, *Boundless Energy* (Rider, 1995)
Dyer, Wayne, W., *Pulling Your Own Strings* (Arrow, 1987)
Graham, Helen, *A Picture of Health: How to Use Guided Imagery for Self-healing and Growth* (Piatkus, 1995)
Kearney, Michael, *Mortally Wounded* (Marino, 1996)
Martin, Philip, *The Zen Path Through Depression* (Harper San Francisco, 2000)
Rowe, Doherty, *Depression: The way out of your prison* (Routledge, NY, 1996)
Siegel, Bernie S., *Love, Medicine and Miracles* (Arrow, London, 1988)
Siegel, Bernie S., *Peace, Love and Healing* (Arrow, London, 1991)
Reber, Arthur, S., (ed.) *Dictionary of Psychology* (Penguin, 1985)
Robertson, Robin, *Introducing Jungian Psychology* (Gill & Macmillan, 1992)
Zweig, Connie and Wolf, Steve, *Romancing The Shadow* (Thorsons, 1997)

B. General Introduction to Meditation:

Dalai Lama (with introduction by Laurence Freeman OSB), *The Good Heart* (Rider, 1996)
Dalai Lama, with Carrière, J-C, *The Power of Buddhism* (New Leaf, 1996)
Dalai Lama, and Cutler, Howard C., *The Art of Happiness* (Hodder & Stoughton, 1998)
Dalai Lama, Ancient Wisdom, *Modern World* (Abacus, 2000)
Osho, *Meditation: The First and Last Freedom* (Newleaf, 1998)
Ozaniec, Naomi, *Teach Yourself Meditation* (Teach Yourself Books, 1987)
Scott, David and Doubleday, Tony, *The Elements of Zen* (Element Books, 1992)

C. Books on Christian Meditation:

Donoghue, John, *Anam Chara* (Bantam, 1997)

Donoghue, John, *Eternal Echoes* (Bantam, 1998)

Freeman OSB, Laurence, *Everyday Christian Meditation* (Hunt & Thorpe, 1994)

Fox, Matthew, *Original Blessing* (Bear & Company, 1983)

Happold, F. C., *Mysticism: A Study And An Anthology* (Penguin, 1990)

Heaney, Marie (ed.), *Letters from Irish People on Sustenance for the Soul* (Town House, 1999)

Holden Capps, Walter and Wright, Wendy M., *Silent Fire: An Invitation to Western Mysticism* (Harper, London, 1978).

Hume OSB, Basil, *Searching for God* (Hodder & Stoughton, 1977)

Johnston SJ, William, *Silent Music: The Science of Meditation* (Fontana, 1974)

Johnston SJ, William, *The Inner Eye of Love* (Fount Paperbacks, 1986)

Johnston SJ, William, *The Mirror Mind* (Fount Paperbacks, 1988)

Johnston SJ, William, *The Wounded Stag* (Fount Paperbacks, 1989)

Johnston SJ, William, *Being in Love: The Practice of Christian Prayer* (Fount, 1989)

Johnston SJ, William, *Arise My Love: Mysticism For A New Age* (Orbis Books, 2000)

Kelsey, Morton, T., *The Other Side of Silence: A Guide to Christian Meditation* (Paulist Press, 1976)

Link SJ, Mark, *Prayer for Beginners and Those Who Have Forgotten How* (Argus, 1976)

Link SJ, Mark, *Vision 2000: Praying Scripture in a Contemporary Way* (Thomas More, 1998)

Link SJ, Mark, *Holy Spirit* (Thomas More, 1998)

Link SJ, Mark, *God The Father* (Thomas More, 1998)

Link SJ, Mark, *Celebrations of Hope* (Thomas More, 1999)

McDonagh, Enda, *The Small Hours of Belief* (Columba, 1989)

Matthews, Caitlín, *Celtic Devotional: Daily Prayers And Blessings* (Gill & MacMillan, 1996)

de Mello SJ, Anthony, *Sadhana: A Way To God* (India, 1985)

de Mello SJ, Anthony, *One Minute Wisdom* (India, 1989)

de Mello SJ, Anthony, *One Minute Nonsense* (India, 1992)

Ní Riain, Nóirín, *Gregorian Chant Experience* (with accompanying CD) (O'Brien Press, 1997)

Okri, Ben, *A Way of Being Free* (Phoenix, 1997)

O'Sullivan SSL, Kathleen, *A Way of Life: A Human-Spiritual Growth Series for Lay Groups* (Veritas, 1987)

Pirola, Teresa, *God in the Ordinary: Reflections on the life of Blessed Edmund Rice* (Christian Brothers, Western Australia, 2000)

Smith, Adrian, B., 'The Spiritual Value of Transcendental Meditation: Prayer' in *Spirituality*, Volume 3, No. 14, Sept/Oct 1997, pp. 304-307.

Smith, Adrian, B., 'The Spiritual Value of T. M.: The Social Dimension' in *Spirituality*, Volume 3, No. 15, Nov/Dec 1997, pp. 359-362.

Taverner, John, *The Music of Silence: A Composer's Testament* (Faber & Faber, 1999)

de Verteuil, Michel, *Eucharist as Word* (Veritas, 2001)

Resources on the Internet

www.sacredspace.ie or www.jesuit.ie/prayer/
    The excellent prayer site of the Irish Jesuits. This site also contains
    many valuable links to other sites of note on prayer.

www.procathedral.ie
    Learn to meditate at the Pro-cathedral, Dublin.

www.homilies.com/mark_link_sj.htm
    A good site dedicated to praying scripture in a contemporary way.

www.dublindiocese.ie
    Has many valuable prayer resources and many excellent links. Probably
    the most valuable site of all.

www.universalis.com
    This is a site dedicated to the Divine Office.

www.wccm.org
    This is a site maintained by the World Community for Christian
    Meditation, spearheaded by Laurence Freeman OSB.

www.karmel.at/ics/others
    A good site on prayer and meditation maintained by the Austrian
    Province of the Teresian Carmel.

www.op.org/domcentral/places/stjude/nineways.html
    This is a site on prayer and meditation maintained by the Dominican
    Order.

www.mcgill.pvt.k12.al.us/jerryd/cm/prayer
    This is a Catholic Web Ring site owed by Jerry Derring. It has a
    plethora of links not alone on prayer, but on practically every aspect of
    faith/theology/spirituality that any Catholic might need.